Gift of ... tt, S.J. ... 955

W9-DIF-577

CARMELITE MONASTERY
LIBRARY
SARANAC LAKE, N Y

THE REFUGE
OF BEAUTY

THE REFUGE OF BEAUTY

A Book of Marian Poems

by

SISTER MARY JULIAN BAIRD, R.S.M.

1954

SAINT ANTHONY GUILD PRESS

Paterson, New Jersey

COPYRIGHT, 1954
BY SAINT ANTHONY'S GUILD, PATERSON, N. J.

Nihil obstat: BEDE BABO, O. S. B.
Censor Librorum

Imprimatur: † JAMES A. McNULTY
Bishop of Paterson

November 5, 1954

PRINTED IN THE UNITED STATES OF AMERICA

TO OUR LADY
OF
A SINGLE ROSE

THE REFUGE OF BEAUTY

This thou hast given us, Mary,
as day dawns darker than night
and all loveliness fades:
in the slender stem of a rose
an impregnable tower;
a shrine to Beauty within
its crimson heart.

CONTENTS

I

[x]

III

Grateful acknowledgement is made to the Catholic Poetry Society of America and to the magazine *America* for permission accorded the author to include in this book "Our Lady of Snow" and "Pieta," which originally appeared in *Spirit* and in *America,* respectively.

I

"One in thy thousand statues we salute thee,
On all thy thousand thrones acclaim and claim...."

— G. K. CHESTERTON

OUR LADY OF SNOW

ALL through her life's close-guarded silences
the secret hours fall —
flake upon flake, each one
a miracle of crystal beauty
formed by master hands —
changing earth's dun to samite where they lie.

A sleeping world wakes not to watch
so still a storm.
Only love lights its little candle
beside a kneeling window and looks out.

And waiting love shall be the first
to see, unveiled, when night is ended,
the hidden glory of Our Lady's grace.

"BLESSED are they who have not seen...."
but who have sought
on mountain paths
your beauty poised
above a winter rose.

"Blessed are they...."
for life shall be for them
this only: your name
and the far music of your smile.

February 11

OUR LADY OF PITY

WELL if one morning
we robe with her pitiful patience,
woven of love and long memories of pain.
Then will the world seem strangely young,
and we be lost to anger.
"Little ones," we shall cry,
"Here is your Mother, come home."

MATER ADMIRABILIS

(To Our Lady of Crimson Slippers)

OUR Lady, wrapt in morning,
prays all quietly,
scarcely aware that some dark prophecy
has dyed her sandals to a scarlet pain.

This sign is for us.

A first red leaf-flame flickers in the undergrowth
of every wood —
mute herald of the whirlwind that will come.
Although days will be deep with summer still
and all the panoply of autumn lies before us,
at last, however late, the conflagration mounts;
the winter's ash is strewn.

REGINA PACIS

PEACE comes to us
as sunset slants through forest leaves,
uncertain ever.

She was enduring day.

DOMINA ANGELORUM

MICHAEL no more leads the heavenly hosts —
strong silver warrior
armed with the lightning's sword —
Michael no more leads the forces of God;
not Michael now, but Mary.

Star-crowned, moon-shod,
brilliant with legions of light massed behind her,
Mary comes forth with no weapon
but a single Word,
and the hordes of hell swarm up
for the last battle.

Rose after rose flames quietly,
and shadows fade
in the soft radiance
of a murmured name.

Soon she shall answer,
shall come as the night wind
to gather all fragrance,
all fire. . . .

O clemens,
O dulcis Maria!

VIRGO POTENS

THOUGH sin might blind the stars,
stifle the sunlight,
web all the winds
in a mesh unbreakable;
her Immaculate Heart alone
could cradle God.

QUEEN OF MARTYRS

THEY brought Saint Stephen's body
to Our Lady,
and she closed her eyes.

O sword of unending sorrow, turning
turning —
O memory!

MATER DOLOROSA

SHE is telling the drop-crystal beads
of the world's wild weeping,
but her fingers caress
the cross of its tears unshed.

MATER AMABILIS

HANDS have held love
all tenderly,
but none like hers.

The one faint mirroring here —
a priest's first Mass.

SEDES SAPIENTIAE

(To Our Lady of Good Counsel)

WISDOM Himself seems well content
within your arms,
nor seeks elsewhere to throne.

Your eyes, His light;
your voice, His speech;
your heart, His love —
till He be grown to stature
at the world's far ending.

April 26

SPECULUM JUSTITIAE

ALL nature mirrors God;
His justice, His holiness;
all loveliness shows forth His limitless beauty,
but she, creation's Queen, mirrors Him best.

Who has known purity
more pure than snow upon her mountaintops —
than lilacs white against her spring's young green?

Hers is the height of peace above the stillest sky
bereft of cloud and bird,
the clearest blue.

All nature mirrors God,
but Mary, best.

PORTENT enough of cruel intent
lay open in Isaias;
surely the Queen of Prophets read aright.

But Bethlehem and baby hands
lulled fears of pain to be,
and Mary shared His sleep of smiling peace.

O brief repose! How soon
old Simeon's rough hand
swept through her web of dreams,
aroused her to words italicized by fire.

First Dolor

THE LOSS IN THE TEMPLE

SHE who has held her God secure
beyond all surety
knows too our fear.

That night of loss
was Mary's nearest step
to hell.

Third Dolor

THERE is centered here
in a woman's tears
and a Man's brave backward glance,
all joy and sorrow, human and divine.

Uncounted Dolor

GRACE BEFORE FRIENDSHIP

Bless us, O Lord!

Thou Who once found in Mary's love
a home;
Who gave, at Cana's feast, the grace of Thy presence,
a token of power divine;
Thou Who on sunlit roads
reveled in children's laughter
and returned their warm embrace!

Lord of the homing heart,
Lord of all graciousness,
Lord of pure joy,
bless us, and these, Thy gifts.

JESUS IS CONDEMNED TO DEATH

THIS is His springtime.
Here a wind of scourging
stirs crimson blooms soon to fall
that we have fruiting.

Pilate, the gardener, sun or rain —
some instrument, not more —
works out the condemnation of Gethsemani
where, in the winter darkness,
a seed died.

First Station

THE WAY OF THE CROSS

WITH a singing heart
to the morning hills
she bore Him,
through Egypt's twilight
stilled Him with lullabies.

Only in this dark climb
is music broken,
and silence sheathes
the sword.

Fourth Dolor

JESUS COMPASSIONATES THE WOMEN
OF JERUSALEM

Now is the Shepherd broken and bound,
led to the slaughter.
(A lamb stirs in the darkness;
the wind is cold.)

"Weep not for Me, but — "
(O night, night,
and the desolate hillsides unprotected!)
" — weep for your children."

Eighth Station

GRADUALLY
we shall grow up to pain
as Mary did.

A sapling set securely by God's hand
withstands the blast
of prophecy, holds out
through exiled dearth
through triple dark,
and in the years serene,
thrusts roots so deep that,
in the great upheaval,
one tree stands.

Fifth Dolor

PIETA

BRING to her arms, mothers of a world long lost,
lovers of all love forever lost,
bring to her heart the silence of your pain.

Noonday may stand beside the cross,
but sorrow bends at evening
above its broken burden
and is still.

No words can touch your anguish.
O let no voice shake the poignant peace of her!
Within the shadow of her patience kneel,
and learn the strength that lets go
all but God, and waits.

Sixth Dolor

ALL that brought joy at Bethlehem
is anguish here.
Yet Mary kneels
till John says, brokenly,
"Mother, the sunset fades...."

Thirteenth Station

THE BURIAL OF CHRIST

SHE watched them roll the stone across
and turned away,
her face as still as snow in winter woods,
but in her eyes
the pain of sunset fires settled
to a single frozen flame
of starred desire:
"In three days He will rise!"

Seventh Dolor

AFTER CALVARY

HERS is no autumn sadness;
summer comes not again
to these darkened hills.

Earth has no season
to match with Our Lady's sorrow,
nor any glory to compare
with her Easter joy.

Seventh Dolor

GOOD FRIDAY NIGHT

THE wild mob was quieter
than this tomb crying "Death";
their angry shouting hurt His Mother
less than Mary's sobbing.

She cannot leave Him to this strident silence:
Who cherished songs at evening,
loved best of all the music of her voice.
That three days' wait will bring
angelic choirs
is only prophecy.
Tonight her Little One
sleeps here alone.

Seventh Dolor

OUR Lady walked alone
from the beginning,
always alone.

And yet,
until He came,
her dark eyes veiled
the anguish of aloofness.
Even in the Afterward
only John saw,
before Communion,
the humble, hungered longing in her glance.

II

"O Jesus, living in Mary, come and live in Thy servants ... in the communion of Thy mysteries...."

— JEAN JACQUES OLIER

DOMUS DOMINI

The Annunciation

NAZARETH was home to her
until an angel voice shook down the stars,
and Love's wings
shadowed the sun.

Heaven and home are one now;
exile is not.
Light dwells within her:
wherever she walks, is God.

March 25

HOW shall she bear that His life
dawn to ineffable morning —
when noon will bring Him death,
and evening a close-sealed tomb?

How endure to lift Him from peace
within her own sweet night
where silent love mutes
all the angels' songs?

How can she think
past pain
to glory?

December 18

CHRISTMAS COMMUNION

WITHIN the soul's dark cavern
love bears Love,
wraps Him in yearning,
and cradles Him in need.

Angels intrude not here,
nor Joseph, nor shepherds;
in the singing silence,
Our Lady kneels alone.

December 25

MORE than the cold
His Mother feels the cut
of disregarded love.

Who later will interpret *Sitio*
as thirst beyond the torment of the body
knows now what makes
her little Jesus weep.

December 25

THE PRESENTATION

SMALL gifts to God
lead on to great.
Our all is never all to Him:
He asks still more.

So Mary with her doves
gave too her Babe
and, after prophecy,
a heart transfixed.

MADONNA OF THE STREET

(*Ferruzzi*)

SEE how His downy head
is snuggled half beneath her hood;
the baby fingers lightly clasp
a fold of her blue cloak;
He is asleep.

But her heart watches ...
The street seems dark to her.
She looks beyond the years
down paths not even saints
have dared to seek —
of grief and fear,
of inexhaustive joy.

When Joseph comes,
she will rouse, and smile
to show him how the little Jesus sleeps.

GETHSEMANI

Not all His night's devotion
poured to a glowing stream of sunset gold,
outshines the star
of this pain-tempered prayer:
"Thy will, not Mine."

"HER body He spared persecution —
Her Passion was just suffering of heart."

Are you quite sure?
Each hissing lash she heard
was martyrdom.

PILATE scarcely guessed
what Mary had always known,
and wondered why
one white-faced woman
knelt.

OFFERTORY:

Jesus Meets His Mother

FIAT for pain,
for dereliction and for death,
was whispered past midnight
from a garden closed.
SUSCIPE, SANCTE PATER. . . .

But farewell to beauty,
chaliced in love within His Mother's eyes,
was raised at noon
above the altar of a crowded street.
OFFERIMUS TIBI, DOMINE. . . .

THE CRUCIFIXION

CALVARY sets curbs
on every grief.

Before such pain
self-pity cannot
stand.

ONLY those who have loved
and been unloved can understand this cry:
the mother of Cain,
the father of the prodigal.
Such love awaits not worded penitence,
nor seeks a sign of sorrow
save the other's need.

First Word

THE RESURRECTION

THERE was a late bird sang
last night
and she heard not.
Let morning's silent jubilee
awake her heart.

No DEEP disguise
could hide Him from
her waiting love.
Before He came
her arms were wide
to welcome Him;
and as dawn burst the tomb of night,
He laid His glory on His Mother's heart.

Easter

THE ASCENSION

ONLY long afterward
John realized
with what renunciation Mary turned
from Heaven's gate to him,
and smiled.

O MARY,
from whom no cloud
but a mist of tears
hid the ascending Christ —
our Lady of Loneliness,
pray for us.

AT NAZARETH
the Breath of God sang softly
for her alone.
Hear now how
a roaring Wind
enwraps the world!

Pentecost

HERE the wind without noise
is the yearning of Christ
in men,
and love flames up and up.

Corpus Christi

THE ASSUMPTION

FIT that her final word
should be an echo
of His own first *Venio*.

THE ASSUMPTION

WHEN Mary came,
God dimmed the lights of Heaven
to a twilight tenderness, remembering
a little Lad run through the evening shadows
to her arms.

God let the twilight deepen into dark
so He could see again, forever,
her face uplifted to Him in His death.

REGINA COELI

THE crown she saw not
for the Hands Which bore it,
and cherished Heaven's diadem no more
than wreaths of flowers twined
by baby Fingers in
far Nazareth.

OUR LADY OF LULLABIES

MUSIC beyond our world's most glorious
thrills her soul now.
Regina Coeli!

But hark, somewhere an earthchild cries
lost and left lonely.
Let angel symphonies be hushed,
the melody of spheres,
for she, unheeding,
sweeps down starsteps,
impatient to soothe his pain.
Maria Mater!

III

"In her is hidden all the sanctity of all the saints."

— THOMAS MERTON

SON OF PERPETUA

OF WHAT strong stuff of sanctity
is this child formed
Who, with wide eyes unafraid
and sturdy little feet
set stubbornly
upon steep slopes,
climbs all alone
to God?

Doubt not the mother heart
that lost this life
in martyrdom
has nourished it in love
to life eternal.

March 6

I HAVE seen
a single birch tree
light
a hill of pines.

April 17

SAINT JOAN OF ARC

NOT now the lily
sheathed in silver steel;
not now the red rose
blown amid flames of hate.

With eyes wide-wondering,
slow, reverent, little feet,
the sweet child-shepherdess from Domremy
goes into Heaven,
bearing field flowers for Mary,
for Him, a new-born lamb.

May 31

SAINT PETER, APOSTLE

EVENING met Peter fleeing from Rome,
evening and Jesus Christ.

Ah, but the morning broke
as he turned back again,
and, for him, there was no night.

June 29

REASSURANCE

HAD Peter stood intrepid,
had he not thrice denied,
would we dare hope
for Pity's instant passing by?

Pardon after the furrowing years
we might expect,
but this glance immediate of love
shatters proud hesitance,
and, going forth, we weep.

SAINT MARY MAGDALENE

MARY was blind that morning,
blind and deaf with grief.
No color of cloud or flower,
no bird song or angel's voice
could hold the heart which sought
incarnate Beauty.

Only when Love called,
only when Love's eyes
lighted her own to glory,
only — ah, miracle —
only then, Mary awoke to life.

July 22

OUR LADY'S MOTHER

As SPRING rains fall
through quiet nights,
and slowly, steadily,
seep to the waiting roots,
so you, forgotten then,
shall bloom in her forever.

July 26

"Put up thy sword"
comes hardly to a soldier.
But as Ignatius laid aside his steel
and took the cross,
the conquest of his army
shook the world.

July 31

SAINT LAWRENCE

WELL might he laugh,
going lonely to difficult death.

Who let pass the world's last riches
in his last friend,
hears in Heaven tonight
the voice of all friends
in One.

August 9

FEAST OF SAINT CLARE

TONIGHT is a woman
whose beauty, veiled in black,
lifts, in a star-jeweled monstrance,
the white moon for Host.

Shadows, like Saracens,
flee instantly;
but mountains
and the singing winds adore.

August 12

MASS OF SAINT ANNE

IN A morning grayer than any we have known,
Anne rose to lay
white vestments for the great Highpriest,
to set upon a secret altar
the golden chalice of His sacrifice.

Hands other than hers will light
the candles she has placed
so high; the censer she prepared
will swing its praises only when she has gone.

This is her Gloria unsung; her service
hidden well away from all but God.

September 8

Because you smile, they will forget
the weariness of soul
that deadened half your days.

We shall remember that,
who climb the same steep spiritual stair,
who share the same dark mystic night.

October 3

THE CHILD MARY GOES TO THE TEMPLE

THIS single streamlet in a desert land,
this one rose on a barren tree —
Anne might have kept her little daughter.

But how then had been wrought
the first link on the silver chain
of sacrifice to save us?
Saint Anne forged it
in the fire of her mother heart.

November 21

TEARLESS, Anne watched her
climb up the temple stairs alone.

Wisdom like hers weeps not
for incense rising,
because for God it burns itself away.

November 21

SAINT FRANCIS XAVIER

THESE two Saint Francis loved in Christ:
Ignatius, and the quest for souls.
And yet he died alone,
with China just beyond.

December 3

WHO knew Love best
felt most love's loneliness;
yet him, of all,
Love last called home.

December 27